Wisdom
FOR LIFE

The personal development devotional filled with inspirational quotes and insights to help you fulfil your potential.

K. A. Atta

ALL RIGHTS RESERVED

This book is copyright under the laws of the United Kingdom. All rightsare reserved. Apart from fair dealing for the purpose of private study,research, criticism or review as permitted under the copyright act, nopart of this publication maybe reproduced, stored in a retrieval system or transmitted in any form or by any means without the prior permission of the copyright owner. All enquiries should be addressed to the publishers.

K. A. Atta
4780 Ashford Dunwoody Road
Suite A-478
Atlanta, GA 30338-5504
USA

T: +1 404 519 4404
wisdom4life@comcast.net

ISBN:141208110-6

Designed in London, England by
Klassicdesign(info@klassicdesign.com)

ACKNOWLEDGMENTS

Dreams do come to pass but never without the help of others. This book would not have been possible without the many people who taught me to change my thinking and to believe in myself. I would first like to thank God for giving me life, and for blessing me with this gift. What a friend you've been!

I also thank Dr. Tayo Adeyemi, founder of New Wine International for the immense help with encouraging me, editing this text and giving me great insight to complete this project. You are a precious gem to this generation, and I can never thank God enough for making our paths cross.

To my spiritual parents, Pastor & Mrs. Frank Ofosu-Appiah, founders of All Nations Church, Atlanta, you have stood with me and believed in me all these years! Thank you for being there for me. You are simply special!

I also thank those practical thinkers and leaders such as John Maxwell, Dr. Myles Munroe, Brian Tracy and Norman Vincent Peale, whose writings have had a great influence on my life.

To Sam and Mary Aikins, thank you for your friendship. Wow, what a journey we've been on! The best is yet to come!

To my parents, Dr. & Mrs. Aboagye-Atta, I say thank you for being there for me, and for the price you paid to get me where I am today.

To my best friend and wife Eno, I say thank you for sharing your precious life with me and for encouraging me keep on running towards the prize. We're in this for the long haul baby!

Finally, but not least, to my precious children, Kaleb and Phoebe; you give me reason to keep doing my best today in order for us to enjoy a better tomorrow. Thank you for being such great friends! I love you!

FOREWORD

Whoever it was that said *"a picture is worth more than a thousand words"* has evidently not read the Lord's prayer; or the 23rd psalm; or Shakespeare; or Lincoln's Gettysburg address; or Winston Churchill's war speeches; or Martin Luther King's "I have a dream."

Charles Osgood said; *"compared to the spoken word, a picture is a pitiful thing indeed"*.

Words are powerful. Words paint pictures that the strokes of a painter's brush know nothing of. Words create and words destroy. Cicero spoke and the people said, "What a wonderful orator"; Demostheises spoke and the people said, "let us march!" That is the awesome power of words.

What you hold in your hands is a powerful compilation of words. Words that will enlighten, enrich, encourage and

empower you. Words that will challenge, inspire and motivate you to greater heights. Words that will ignite a fresh fire in your soul and cause your mind to explode with new
possibilities. Words that will create new horizons for your eyes and open up new vistas before you. Words that will draw out your latent abilities and expose your raw potential. Words that will propel you towards your goals with incredible momentum.

Now this is not one of those books that you read once and put down when you have finished it. No, this is not a book you can finish.

I recommend that you use it like a bottle of vitamins for your mind. Read a portion each day, every day. And when you come to the end, start again.

The words on some pages will dance out of the page and

burn in your heart. Mark those pages for quick reference.

As you do this, you will find that you are giving yourself instructions. The amazing thing is you never know when you will need to use those instructions. But when the time comes you will be ready.

Konrad Adenauer said; "we all see the same sky, but we don't all have the same horizon".

Welcome to a new horizon!

Dr Tayo Adeyemi
CEO, New Wine International

INTRODUCTION

Many have simply misunderstood the entire concept of personal success and their role in making this a reality. Personal success and excellence do not just happen. They are sought after earnestly with measured effort and strategy in all instances, without exception.

This devotional is loaded with nuggets of wisdom that will certainly challenge your thinking to help you discover the person you were created to be. Without this discovery, your life can never be lived to its fullest potential, and you will never know how great you could have become.

I have seen too many people sit and wait for something good to come their way, when they have all the time been the only catalyst and vehicle capable of bringing their desires to pass.

You are simply too loaded to stay where you are, and in the situations you find yourself in. You can achieve that dream and live your life with deliberate intent.

It is my earnest hope that the truths presented in this book will energize you enough to the point of taking action to effect positive change in your life. If you are ready to leverage yourself to greatness, and to maximize your potential, then this book is for you.

Norman Vincent Peale once said, *"Become a possibilitarian. No matter how dark things seem to be or actually are, raise your sights and see possibilities - always see them, for they're always there."*

Make it happen!

This book is dedicated to all those out there who believe that nothing can stop them from achieving their dream. Pursue!

Success is not automatic. It is the result of a pragmatic process that combines hard work, determination, failure and commitment.

I once heard someone describe 'man' as one who is *'engineered'* for success. I like that description very much. But as much as we are 'engineered' to succeed, success is not automatic. A car is designed to move but be sure that this will not happen till you get behind the wheel, turn the ignition and start moving the car. Success does not come through wishful thinking. It comes rather from wilful thinking and action. Whatever you desire to accomplish in life will only happen if you purposefully pursue your dreams with measured and sustained effort. Even failure is essential to experience success. Do not despise your mistakes but learn from them and begin more intelligently. Begin to run purposefully, and you will achieve that dream. Zig Ziglar said *"You were born to win, but to be a winner, you must plan to win, prepare to win, and expect to win"*. If it is to be, it's up to you.

Purpose is the 'why-you-were-made', which was determined before you were thrust into existence.

None of us was born without a purpose in Life, as purpose is always established before creation. The reason for the existence of a thing determines the design process, which is fundamental in any creation process. A telephone was created to enable two people talk to each other from two different locations; and this is the governing purpose that determined its design. And within its design is embodied the ability to fulfil this purpose. It is the same with us. Each of us has been endowed with special abilities for the achievement of our purpose. But first, we must know and understand our purpose. When we know our purpose, we will stop living to please others. Next, we will begin to tap into the incredible resources God has placed within us. Wherever you find yourself in life, it's never too late to begin!

The day I realised that I did not have to live in any situation I did not approve of, I entered a new dimension of power. I realised that I had the power to choose to do something about my life.

Henry David Thoreau (1817 – 1862, American Essayist, Poet) made a remarkable statement and said, *"I know of no more encouraging fact than the unquestionable ability of man to elevate his life by conscious endeavour."* When you come to the point where you discover the immense treasures of abilities within you, suddenly almost everything becomes possible. You break free to become the master of your destiny. You realise that choice more than chance will bring you your desired successes. Today may be the right time to question and challenge your values and actions. Are you doing what you ought to be doing? Are you happy with where you are in Life now? Most importantly, are you heading to a place of your choice, or one by default? If not, make up your mind, not tomorrow, not later, but NOW, to live a better life. Your life is really for living.

**Think outside the box;
Step out of your comfort zone;
Stay ahead of the game.**

Thinking outside the box denotes creativity and proactivity. Stepping out of your comfort zone denotes courage and boldness. Staying ahead of the game denotes persistence and sheer tenacity. These are the essential attributes to getting ahead and staying ahead in Life. If you wait for things to happen before you act, you are not being proactive; if you allow fear of failure to grip you and keep you in your comfort zone, you will never know greatness; and if you do not develop the guts to strategically negotiate your way through Life, you will never know *'what might have been.'* Take steps towards that goal for unless you try to do something beyond what you have already mastered, you will never grow.

Your world is designed to change continually, whether or not you choose to change it. But you possess the power to determine its direction.

In Life, change is the only permanent thing. From birth, we begin to change, and so do the things that concern us. We were however created to be proactive about our lives, and we have within us, the ability to direct our lives to accomplish our purpose. If you choose not to do this, Life will unfold to you in a random fashion and make of you what it pleases. But when you live by your own design, you can make your efforts steer you to a port of your choice. Today, purpose in your heart to regain control over every part of your life you have lost control over. It may be your dream or your willingness to fight. Rise up and confront Life and be the winner you were created to be.

Each moment that passes is vital to the attainment of your goals and vision. Learn to be accountable for each passing moment, and in so doing your days.

It is said that a journey of a thousand miles begins with a step. In the same way, the *'journey to become'* consists of moments within which we must 'do' in order to 'be'. Each of these moments grants us a medium, within which we can do something in order to become the person we desire, or to attain that to which we aspire. One of our biggest problems is, we get so caught up with the big picture, and forget that to live our dream would require us dealing wisely with our little moments. Avoid the illusion of waiting for that 'big moment' to arrive, with its embedded impetus for action. What matters is what you do with those fleeting moments, which are here now, but alas, gone in an instant. Lord Chesterfield (British Statesman 1674 – 1773) said, *"I recommend that you take care of the minutes, for the hours will take care of themselves."*

Your dream must be strong enough to get you back on your feet when life knocks you down.

What will it take to stop you? Think about that for a moment…. How persistent are you? Is your dream big enough, vital enough that you are willing to confront Life when it brings you something you did not order? Is it big enough to make you forget the shameful mistakes you made in your past and fight again? Will it fade in the midst of trials? The journey to fulfil purpose involves many 'knock-downs' and in times like these, there has to be something within you that makes you want to get back up and keep running. Tobias Wolff rightly said, *"We are made to persist; and that's how we find out who we are."* Again, I ask you, "What will it take to stop you?"

To be effective, you must prioritise your activities into the following order of importance:

> **Must do**
> **Should do**
> **Nice to do**

We live in days where the 24-hour day, for some strange reason, seems to be getting shorter for most people. Lack of time is known to be one of our biggest complaints. But isn't it interesting to note that time has not ceased to daily deposit the same 86,400 seconds into our accounts? Time cannot be expanded. It can only be 'created' within itself by taking from one activity to give to another. But how do we distribute our daily time quota effectively? Know the difference between 'the urgent' and 'the truly important'. The truly important things in Life are those that influence our long term goals and vision. Urgent things are not necessarily unimportant, but can become a distraction when not managed properly. Learn to develop a To-Do list for your daily activities, and their priorities must be allocated according to 'Must Dos', 'Should Dos', and 'Nice to Dos'.

Daring the 'impossible';
breaking the status quo;
dancing to your own tune;
always pressing forward;
That's the way to success.

Dare to be different! Get some good old-fashioned courage and make a move in the right direction. Quit living your life on the terms of others, and organising your life around the expectations of people. Life will not happen to you as you wish, except by what you demand. I have seen too many people loaded with potential and great ideas but had no courage to take steps to make those dreams come to pass. If you are going to be truly successful, you have to break free from the limitations of people and the society. Re-analyse what is known as common truth and traditions. They could be holding you back. If you find yourself in any such situation, do not be afraid to break free. You must live your life on your terms; and this is your only chance at it!

You can never care more about the goal than you do the process.

We have lived so long in a culture that has taught us to be satisfied by merely stating our resolutions or goals without a plan or process of how to achieve them. The result is the many people we see walking around with a picture of a better life but without a clue of how to make that become reality. One of the most important things to know is that 'process' is what ratifies the authenticity of the goal. Without it, your goal is worthless. When you plan, you lay out the sequence of events that have to occur for you to achieve your goal. Your process or plan is the only bridge between where you are and where you intend to get to. Do you have a road map or plan to make you achieve your dream? Plan on paper and review constantly till you get to your destination.

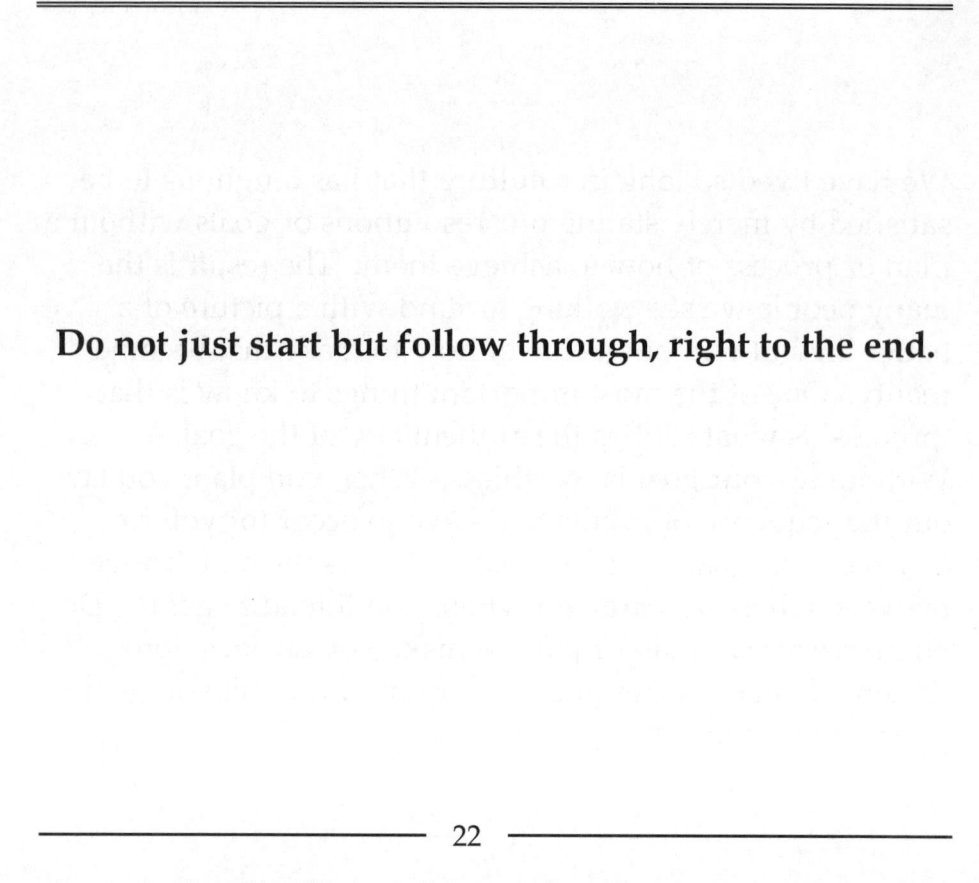

Do not just start but follow through, right to the end.

Wisdom for Life

The wayside of Life is full of people who started something in a spurt but lacked the stamina to finish. I do believe that starting an endeavour is as good as half—done; but do not stop when seemingly insurmountable challenges flare up. You can outgrow every challenge that life throws at you if you push hard enough. Your willingness to persist in the face of every adversity can be your greatest asset. When you build the discipline to keep fighting, you develop the inner strength and tenacity to bulldoze your way through Life. Gerry Harvey (Australian Businessman) once said *"I went to the brink many times. A couple of times I thought 'I'm gone. This is it.' But then I would just keep working. I think if you're close to the brink and just make sure that you work twice as hard and put twice as much effort into everything and the people around you and everything, you should come through.*

Discover yourself, know yourself and then master yourself.

Benjamin Franklin, (Former American Scientist and Diplomat) once made a profound statement. He said, *"there are three things extremely hard: steel, a diamond, and to know one's self."* It is truly difficult, yet necessary. A man who does not know himself will never understand his limitations, his potential or his purpose. It is also said that before a man can wake up and find himself famous, he has to first wake up and find himself! Someone once said that, *"Every one of us has in him a continent of undiscovered character. Blessed is he who acts the Columbus to his own soul"*. However, discovering your potential does not make you successful; it is only the beginning. A friend of mine recently made a stunning statement when he said, "Success consists in being successful, not in having potential for success." From now on, place a demand on yourself to discover yourself, and then use that potential to bring lasting success, whatever it takes.

The greatest assassin to your aspirations is to see yourself through the eyes of other people.

Every one of us has an inherent need to be appreciated and feel accepted. The trouble with this is when you allow it to dominate your desires to the point that it becomes your motive for service, action and friendship. You then willingly compromise your personal values in an effort to feel accepted by others. When you do this, you inadvertently abandon your own dreams and only become concerned with living to other people's standards and opinions. Consequently, you begin to measure yourself to this image you see through the eyes of other people, but somehow never seem to measure up. Do not allow other people's opinion of you to become your reality or focus. Don't allow yourself to be another pawn in someone else's pursuits for they will give you up at the earliest opportunity if it serves their interests better. Be content with yourself for there is none other like you. Enjoy your uniqueness.

We should make choices that will fill our minds with pleasant memories of the past, a purposeful present and a hopeful future.

We are where we are today primarily due to the choices we have made in the past. We are in the relationships we find ourselves in because we choose to. Our hope or hopelessness for the future is because of the choices we made yesterday that culminated in our situations and feelings today. Life does and will always happen from us. This is why we must begin to realise the potency of our decisions and choices, so we can look forward to a hopeful future based on a purposeful present.

Refuse to blame someone else for where you are now. Blame only releases you from facing the awesome responsibility of choosing to liberate your future by conscious endeavour. What has happened in your past and what is happening to you now are tiny matters compared to what you choose to do about them. It is always in your response!

Recognising an opportunity is one thing. Maximizing its benefits is another thing altogether.

If you were walking down the street and noticed a fifty-dollar note on the floor, you would probably bend down to pick it up, right? Or, if you stood beneath a mango tree with many ripe fruit, no matter how much you desired the fruit, you would have to grab a stick or a stone, in order to pluck one off the branch. In both cases, you would have to take action to get a result right? Life expresses itself through action! Action is the link between recognizing opportunities and reaping its benefits, while commitment to the goal is the fuel that keeps you going. Our progress in life is never blocked by what we want to do and can't, but by what we ought to do and don't! By all means, take time daily to dream, but please do not stop there. There comes a time when you have to stop being the architect and become the bricklayer!

Having an attitude of gratitude will go a long way to determine your altitude.

A man looked into the eyes of his son and said, *"If someone you knew were to give you a million dollars, and tell you to spend it anyway you want, what would be the first thing you would buy?"* "That's easy," his son replied, "I'd buy a Thank You card!" This is a person with an attitude of gratitude. I wonder how many of us would have given the same answer. I would probably have thought about my first debt-free mansion! There is something about an attitude of gratitude that never allows worry and anxiety to come close. The more you cultivate the habit of gratitude, the better your outlook on Life will be; and the better your outlook on Life is, the greater your drive and expectation in Life will be. Begin to cultivate an attitude of gratitude and there is no limit to how high you will rise in Life.

The "this-is-how-things-are-done" syndrome is the greatest inhibitor of human potential. It is called "status-quo."
Break free and live!

The struggle between conformity and individuality is one we constantly face. Every choice we make and every action we take, takes us deeper into conformity or more towards the lonely road of individuality. When we succumb to the status quo, we lose our individuality. 'Status quo' insists that we behave in a particular manner, tells us what we can and cannot do, and denies us the knowledge of the freedom to choose to do what we desire. When we conform to the status quo, we relinquish our identity by following the crowd and therefore deny the world of our potentially unique contribution. Instead of conforming to the status quo, choose rather to conform to the image of the person you desire to become, and to sound principles. The world is waiting with bated breath for the release of your potential!

The key to effective time management is this; you must determine what is worthy of your attention and what is not.

We are living in times where it is very easy for other things to distract us from pursuing the truly important things we set out to do. Have you ever planned your day but never managed to get anything done because other 'unplanned' issues surfaced and you had to attend to them? Everyone has. But if you are going to get effective in time management, the first rule is simple: Learn to say NO! Everything you do that requires your time represents a choice. This is fact. Our reluctance to refuse to do things that are not important causes us to waste our time. I am not implying that every unplanned event that arises is a waste of time. You may not be in total control of that. Rather, you must know how to sift through the happenings of the day in order to identify and separate the urgent from the truly important.

You must employ extra care not to allow your failures and past experiences to distort the way you perceive life. For if your perception is wrong, you will define situations wrongly.

Having the right perception in any situation is very important as it determines what your next action will be. I have developed the habit of seeing every failure that comes my way as a learning process and a necessary step towards pursuing success in Life. Perception has to be built on true principles and lasting values, and not a weak foundation of past emotional experiences. In this way, you are able to make right choices about every situation you encounter. A wrong perception can cost you great opportunities to succeed in Life. How do you perceive Life? Eleanor Roosevelt said, *"A stumbling block to the pessimist is a stepping-stone to the optimist."* Are you always looking on the negative side of things? Have you given up on succeeding in Life because your wrong perceptions about your past failures have dampened your desires? Get a true perspective of your perceptions and make that necessary change. You really can do it.

Your attitude to Life will always be affected by the company you keep.

It is said that where we find ourselves in five years time is directly affected by the books we read and the friends we keep. The importance of maintaining friends who are not there just for the glamour but will help lift you to your place of prominence can never be over-emphasised. Iron sharpens iron while any other material rubbed against the iron makes it blunt with time. So it is in relationships. Any relationship with a person who does not operate on the same or higher frequency with you is excess weight you can do without. Many people find this issue uncomfortable for many reasons and convince themselves that they can *tolerate* some relationships while pursuing their vision. But there comes a time when you have to make that intelligent but painful decision to leave some people behind and become the eagle you were created to be. Now may be that perfect time.

Unless we rise up, come to the realisation that 'the place where we dwell is too strait for us,' and make that intelligent decision to take steps to increase and enlarge ourselves spiritually, financially, emotionally and mentally, come next year, we shall be where we are now having made absolutely no progress.

Wishing for progress in one's life and rising up to make things happen are two entirely different things. Many times we come to places of intense dissatisfaction with our achievements and circumstances but stop there. Some find the effort required for change too much to give or the risks involved too high to contemplate. Others find change fearful and rather choose to settle for the little comfort they have acquired in their lives. But without the willingness to take risks, nothing extraordinary is going to happen in your life. Till you let go of what you hold in your hands today for the sake of a better tomorrow, life will continue to be one drab and uneventful experience. Remember that anything unattempted remains impossible. Begin to set goals and devise a plan that will bring total satisfaction in every area of your life. Your life must be lived at all cost! You only have one chance at it.

When we dwell on worrying about our future, we relinquish the power we possess in the present to order our future, and look forward to a future which dwells on chance.

The best way to predict the future is to create it, not by a magical wave of the hand but by careful planning, persistent action and unbreakable resolve. This is faith in action. When we worry about the future, we begin to give life to our fears. And like faith, fear can be worked to produce its undesirable fruits. When fear is in action, it blinds us of the opportunities we possess in our present to sow the seeds for a greater tomorrow. The future can not be predicted in its entirety, but you can sure guide it in the direction you want it to go by right choice and action today. Do not leave your future to chance; you can really live your life by design.

You must be willing to cross the line of your safety zone if you're going to enter greatness. Without the willingness to take high risks, you will dwell in mediocrity.

Anyone aspiring to live a successful life must be willing to break out of the confines of their familiar situations and environment. Nature teaches us a wonderful lesson in the development of a butterfly that if we want to fly badly enough, we must be willing to give up being a caterpillar. Living within your comfort zone is like being caged by your fears. Your fearful anticipation of what could happen if you gave up your current comforts, keeps you locked up. If you are going to make it, you must be willing to take risks; give up what you have now and take a giant leap on the wings of hard work to a successful life. Do not fear what could happen if something went horribly wrong. Be afraid rather that your life will never begin!

We tend to get what we expect even if we expect nothing.

To expect is to look forward to or wait for something. When we expect something, we prepare for its arrival or we plan to accomplish something. So when we expect to win, we employ a strategy that will make us win. On the other hand, when we expect nothing, we act accordingly by doing nothing as it takes nothing to receive nothing. Expectation is a powerful force that releases energy or action into your life. Begin to be expectant in life and you will be amazed at the purposefulness that will be released into your life. Dennis Waitley once said; *"Our limitations and successes will be based, most often, on our own expectations for ourselves. For what the mind dwells upon, the body acts upon."*

Where do you want to be tomorrow? Decide. How do you intend to get there? Plan. What next? Take the first step and keep on keeping on till you arrive at your destination.

We all go through this three-step process in our everyday activities. If anyone of these steps is missing or ineffective, it affects the result. Once you decide to maximise your life, you must plan in no uncertain terms how you intend to accomplish this feat. Set meaningful goals and begin to take steps, one at a time, towards your goal. Don't just set resolutions; go on from there and plan. It is said that *'Planning is bringing the future into the present so that you can do something about it now.'* The strength of a firm decision coupled with a good plan will release the motivation to help you keep on till you achieve your purpose.

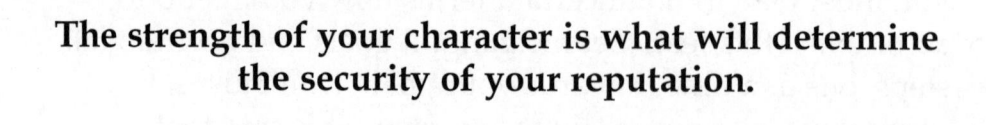

The strength of your character is what will determine the security of your reputation.

Wisdom for Life

The most gracious pursuit anyone could embark on is the development of good character. Unfortunately, our society has mostly taught us to pursue our aspirations, careers and to gain public victories without building the foundations that will bring satisfying and lasting success. Character is that foundation which many have overlooked or simply not bothered to do anything about. We are not born with it. It is something we form by careful chipping through our thoughts and choices. Michelangelo once said *"I saw the angel in the marble and carved until I set him free"*. The gems we possess are within. Set them free! From today, determine to make decisions based on true character. Mean what you say; deliver what you promise; think good thoughts; engage in worthy pursuits; deal honestly, and do onto others as you would want others to do onto you!

You have to consciously and purposefully pursue your dreams with calculated and sustained effort, in order to bring your dreams to reality.

Most people I have met do have a dream of something they want to achieve but somehow lack the right strategy and energy to bring them the corresponding result. Vaclav Havel (Former Czech President) once said *"Vision is not enough. It must be combined with venture. It is not enough to stare up the steps; you must step up the stairs."* If you are going to see your dreams materialise, you have to have a dynamic, written plan which must be reviewed constantly as your needs and circumstances change. The results you achieve will always be in proportion to the effort you apply and the effectiveness of the plan you adopt. Always remember that. And above this, you must determine to hold on, no matter what, till your dream materialises.

A person's attitude and behaviour is a reflection of his dominant thoughts. For as a man thinketh, so is he.

Our thoughts have an effect on virtually every aspect of our lives. You have to understand that you cannot think in one way and act in another. The two go together. All our actions spring from our thoughts. In other words, action is a blossom of thought which then leads to the results we enjoy, fondly remember or regret. Henry David Thoreau (Former American Essayist) once said; *"Thought is the sculptor who can create the person you want to be!"*

Every thought you entertain has an effect on your being and character. Each thought continually chips and moulds the person you are becoming. You cannot afford to be on autopilot and let your thoughts rule your life and determine how you turn out. Rather, direct your thoughts to create the person of character you intend to become.

Our words are powerful. The man who has discovered this wealth and uses it wisely shall never be poor.

The words we speak are life. Have you realised that when you continually say good things about yourself, others and situations, they change for the better? Whether we believe it or not, we will always reap the fruits of our confessions. After affirmation comes realization. In John 1:14, we read that *"And the Word became flesh and lived…"* Drawing a perfect analogy between this scripture and our confessions, we realise that the end result of our words is the bearing of its fruit. If you find yourself stuck in a rut of negative confessions, break that destructive cycle and begin to sow some seeds of positive life. You must purpose in your heart to keep watch over every word that comes out of your mouth because the end result of your words is life. Don't give life to what you do not want.

Attitude is key to your success.

Have you ever met one of those people who never got on with anybody and found everything wrong with every job they had after only a couple of weeks? People, whose attitude was so bad that every situation they found themselves in, seemed to turn against them? Eric Butterworth said *"Attitudes are the forerunners of conditions."* And he could not have been more right. Your attitude to life goes before you and will either open doors or shut your eyes to opportunities ahead. There comes a time when you need to sit yourself down and do some serious soul-searching when you can't seem to hold on to any relationship or job. It could be an attitude problem. The good thing is that attitudes are developed and are subject to change. If you find yourself under the burden of a wrong attitude, it's never too late. Make that change now!

When you enjoy the process, you stay inspired and motivated. This is the key to continuous productivity and effectiveness.

It is very easy to stay motivated when you enjoy what you do; and when you are motivated in life, achieving your dream is relatively easy. I realise that the reason so many people are unhappy is because they employ the wrong process to achieve a particular goal. The process should not be a means to an end but the means to the end. A wrong process has embedded within it, a bundle of frustration, and it is like trying to climb a mountain with a pair of sneakers. When you apply the right tactics and methods, you will see results. And when you see results, you get motivated. And when something keeps you motivated, you enjoy it.

Weak decisions always lead to wrong choices.

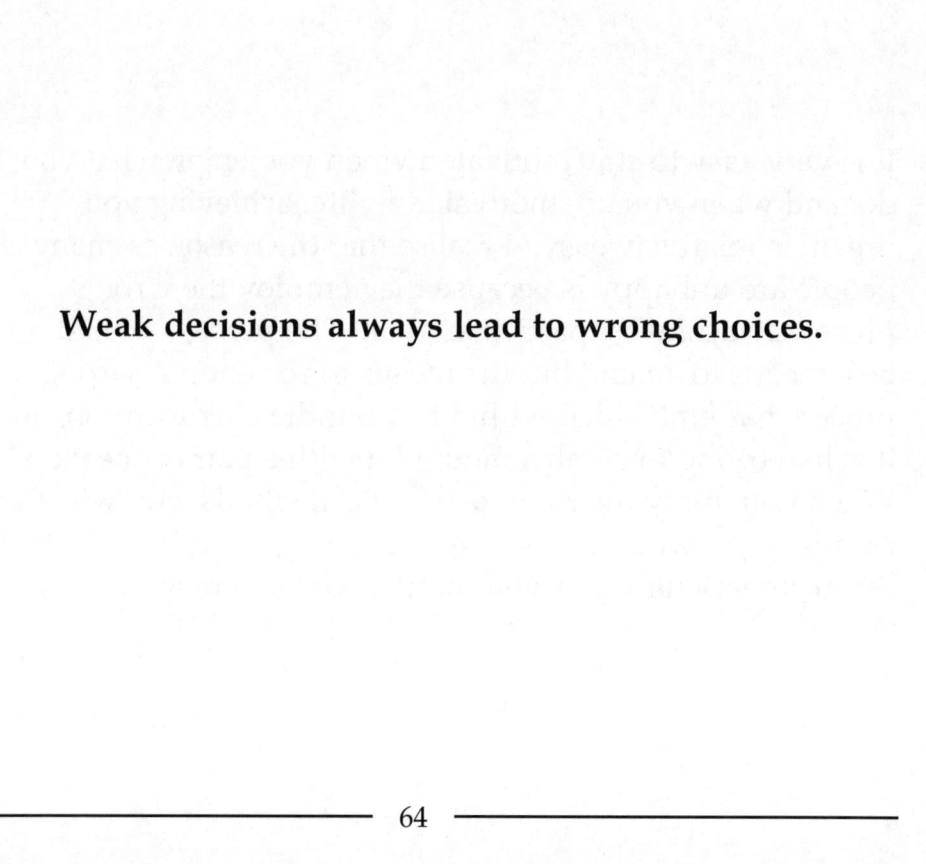

To make a decision is to draw a conclusion or make a verdict about something, based on your knowledge of it. When a decision is made, you make choices congruent with it. When you decide to break a habit without finding out the things that help reinforce it, you are bound to make a weak decision. A weak decision can still be influenced by some other opinion, suggestion or feeling. This implies that you will make your choices based on how you feel at the time and not on the decision. This leads to fickle choices. So before you make a decision about anything, make it a point to first understand what the situation involves, so you can make the right choices.

Brooding over failure leads to self-pity and there is no greater self-destructive habit than self-pity.

One of the greatest misconceptions about failure has to do with people seeing themselves as failures after they fail in an attempt to accomplish a feat. You have to understand that failure is an event that is necessary to experience before success. If you tolerate this mistaken belief that you are a failure, self-pity will set in, which will then take away the desire to try again. John W. Gardener (American Educator) once said, *"Self-pity is easily the most destructive of the non-pharmaceutical narcotics; it is addictive, gives momentary pleasure and separates the victim from reality."* I believe there is nothing more dangerous than that which causes one to give up trying. Take your finger off the self-destruct button and give yourself another chance. Keep trying, until.

Anyone can coast downhill when the going is easy and comfortable. But only those with an unwavering desire to succeed in life can trudge uphill and accommodate discomfort without losing sight of their vision.

If you are going to make it in life, you will need to build persistence into your character. Life is full of twists and turns, hills and valleys. The journey is never straight, nor does the road wind through flowery parks and peaceful lanes only. Tough and unfavourable situations do come to everyone, while many of the situations we face have the ability to knock our much-needed breath out of us. You have to be of those who can accommodate discomfort while pursuing success. Successful people never allow their failures and difficult situations to stop them. They understand that tough and determined people outlive every problem. They also know that no one else holds the keys to their vision but themselves; and until they give in to the pressures of life, they will make it. Stand out from the masses.

Do not be concerned about who is against you or who is not on your side. Worry rather about time. That is what you don't have on your side. From the moment you breathed your first breath of fresh air, time started to run out. Maximise therefore, every moment you have.

Many people spend their time finding ways in which to please others. Such is their need for acceptance that they forget about the most important commodity available to man, time. You have a set time within which to achieve your purpose. Each moment you live counts towards the attainment of your purpose and goals; and each moment you live is a unit of your life spent, forever! From this day forward, purpose in your heart to be a good steward of time. Be accountable first to yourself on how you spend time. Have this sense of urgency but enjoy life as well! Henry Twells (1823-1900) reflected on the value of time and wrote, "When as a child I laughed and wept, time crept. *When as a youth I waxed more bold, time strolled. When I became a full-grown man, time RAN. When older still I daily grew, time FLEW! Soon I shall find in passing on, time gone!"* Do it now!

Bitterness is as sure to destroy your health and well-being as any other known vice. Many do not understand the destructive powers of this evil. But no matter how far you stay away from it, you are still only one offence from being held in its powerful grip.

One of my mentors once said to me in a counselling session that 'bitterness is like drinking poison and expecting the person you are bitter against to be hurt.' That is exactly the power of this evil. It has the power to poison your very body physically. It has been proven scientifically that harbouring ill feelings about someone can have a harmful effect on your health. There is no time like NOW to rid yourself of any bitterness in your heart. If you can't give it up, seek help today before it runs its full course and destroys you. Harry Emerson Forsdick, a former American Clergyman once said, *"Bitterness imprisons life; love releases it. Bitterness paralyzes life; love empowers it. Bitterness sours life; love sweetens it. Bitterness sickens life; love heals it. Bitterness blinds life; love anoints its eyes."*

Every adversity or unfavourable situation that comes your way is designed to change you. But you determine the change by your response.

= Wisdom for Life

It is said that tough times don't last, only tough people do. We are subject to change everyday of our lives by the external influences we encounter. We have no control over the things that happen to us but we have every inch of control over how we respond to them. Thomas Edison, one of the greatest inventors that ever lived lost his New Jersey laboratories to a fire in 1914. Valuable records of his experiments and $2million worth of equipment lost. On assessing the damage, the 67 year- old Edison said *"There is great value in disaster. All our mistakes are burned up. Thank God we can start anew!"* What an attitude to life! Lena Horne (Actress and Singer) once said, *"It is not the load that breaks you down, it's the way you carry it."* If you choose the right response, you will outgrow it.

Every man has within, a luxury, a priceless gem that money could not buy nor replace. It is the ability to choose.

The ability to choose is man's most basic freedom. If you take away a man's ability to choose what he wants to do, when he wants to do it, he loses his freedom. Choice is the freedom to opt for one thing over another. You can choose what you want from life by being proactive. As a matter of caution, never make choices based on habit and reaction. Never make choices to please someone as you end up being the loser. Your ability to choose is so priceless, and you can employ it to steer you to a haven of your own design. One writer wrote so eloquently and said, *"There is a choice you have to make in everything you do. And you must keep that in mind; the choice you make, makes you."* Choose wisely.

Focusing on your failures will only help in holding you back from achieving your potential. Learn that every true winner has scars most people cannot identify with.

A misconception about failure can potentially harm your drive to achieve success. Many view their scars, for example, a business that went bust, as confirmation of the fact that they are failures. No! Scars, though ugly, should be used as reasons for pressing on and NOT stations to park your dreams. Your greatest glory is not in never falling, but in rising every time you fall. When you focus negatively on your failures, you irresponsibly take your eyes off your strengths and focus on your weaknesses. Realise that only you can identify with your scars, and no one else. So do not accept the negative things people say about your failures. Start over again for you now know more than you did when you made the earlier attempt. I know it may mean becoming a laughing stock sometimes but I know this one thing; success never shied away from the persistent person. There still remains much more to be won.

Forget about trying to get everyone to understand you. Forget about trying to explain yourself to people why you made your mistakes. Forget about trying to get everyone to love you. It won't work.

One thing you have no control over is what people choose to think about you. People may see you through the eyes of your past or through their perception of who you are. So even though you may be a different person now, achieving greater things, their opinion of you may revert to what they know you to be. It's called familiarity, and it is your greatest enemy to making progress in a known environment. Forget it; you cannot change anyone's mind about you. It is their prerogative to choose to see you differently. Fortunately, that has no effect on you. If you are bogged down with what other people think about you, it's time to break free from it. There is nothing you can do about it. What you can do something about is you and how you see yourself! One philosopher once said, *"Be who you are and say what you feel, because those who mind don't matter, and those who matter don't mind."* Could he have been more right?

How you see yourself is key to your success.

Eleanor Roosevelt once said; *"No one can make you feel inferior without your consent,"* and there is some truth in that. No one can value you less than the value you place on yourself. If you have great self-esteem, it shows in your actions, your drive and how you communicate. Your self-esteem is a measure of how much value you place on yourself. Those with a high level of self-esteem are not arrogant! Their actions are simply a reflection of their 'can-do' mentality. There is an energy around people who see themselves as capable of overcoming every challenge. Doors seem to open for such people and they overcome every struggle. How do you see yourself? If you were asked to describe yourself in a sentence, what words would you use? Think highly of yourself, for the world takes you at your own estimate.

He that knows the value of time has the key to personal effectiveness.

The ability to manage one's time is the key to personal effectiveness. Knowing the value of time adds a sense of urgency and purpose to your life. Time, in essence, is the unit of measurement of life. So when you learn to be accountable for your time, you in effect become accountable for your life. You cannot live a fruitful life without being a good steward of time. Time is like money, which can either be spent or invested. I find it quite interesting to note that most people only care about how much return they make on a financial investment without caring about how much return they make on the time invested in various activities. Till you value your time, you will continue to waste those precious moments laden with opportunities to make the life you want happen to you. Remember that the quality of your life will largely be determined by how you use and manage your time.

Where you will be tomorrow depends on the choices and decisions you make today.

You are where you are today by virtue of your choices yesterday, and the results of your choices are what you are enjoying or regretting today. Life happens from us, and what we do today has a bearing on what we experience tomorrow. Do not take lightly your decisions and choices, for they bear within them the seed of the fruit we shall either enjoy or regret tomorrow. Dwight Eisenhower, former president of the USA once said, *"The history of free men is never really written by chance but by choice; their choice!"* From today, make wise choices that will make you look on your yesterdays with fond memories and your future with hope.

Power resides in the ability to choose. Therefore use your power to make choices that will take you where you ought to be – On Top!

James Allen (Author of 'As a man thinketh' 1864 – 1912) said, *"Man is made or unmade by himself. By the right choice he ascends… and as Lord of his own thoughts, he holds the key to every situation."* When we exercise our power to choose, we eliminate ourselves from receiving what Life gives out by default. We take the reins of our future and begin to activate the seeds of our creative abilities. We then receive what we expect, which is the true value of our identity. Denis Waitley once said, *"There are two primary choices in life; to accept conditions as they exist, or accept the responsibility for changing them."* Make choices that will bring you the fruits you desire. You have the power to do it.

If you constantly look for the approval of others, how can you keep your eyes on your vision? You are bound to miss it.

We are not designed to focus on different things at the same time. In order to focus on something, you have to take your eyes off some other thing. When you keep seeking attention and approval from others, you lose your individuality. Worse still, you lose sight of your vision and dreams. And when this happens, you become very dissatisfied with life. Have you realised how much you begin to hate yourself when someone you lived to please suddenly walked out on you? Do not let someone's opinion of you become your reality. Believe in yourself and quit seeking approval from people. Your life is way too precious to live it on someone else's terms. They will forget about you anyway, when you are gone.

It has been proved scientifically that there is a direct correlation between our minds, concepts, and our actions. Our actions are merely reflections of our dominant thoughts.

Our thoughts are reflected in our attitude to life, which then reflects in our actions. Action therefore is the best interpreter of our thoughts. I am sure you are familiar with the principle of thought and action, which says that *'as a man thinketh in his heart, so is he.'* In other words, as you think, so you act. It is important to understand this principle so you know how to halt certain habits and trends in your life. If you desire to see some constructive action in your life, begin to think some constructive thoughts regarding the same. If you want to break a bad habit, do not reinforce it by thinking about how dominating it is over you. Rather, see yourself walking free and doing the exact thing you desire to start doing, and it will manifest.

In order to win, you must expect to win. For indeed this is one of the most basic principles of achievement; expectation precedes realization.

Winning in life does not come to everyone, though it is available to everyone. There are principles or forces we must employ to see our lives become what they were designed to be. One of these is expectation. It is such a powerful force that makes seemingly insurmountable mountains become like molehills. Real winners face every situation with one thing in mind – to triumph and get to the other side victorious. They expect to win! They refuse every result contrary to their expectation. Begin to expect what you desire, for many times, this is the missing link between your desires and their realization. Eric Butterworth once said of expectation: *"Faith is expectancy. You do not receive what you want; you do not receive what you pray for, not even what you say you have faith in. You will always receive what you actually expect."*

It is not wise to build an altar at your failures and mourn yourself to self-pity. Shake the dust off and press on. More battles remain to be won.

We have all been through the stage in life where as little children, we tried to take our first steps but fell down after a couple of steps. Even if you do not remember your experiences during this time, you may have seen your own children or other children go through this. Have you realised that when they fall, they laugh, and try to step out again? That's the attitude we need to adopt in life. When we fail in an attempt to achieve something, let us rise up again, for there remains everything to gain and a purpose to achieve. Thomas Edison made over a thousand attempts in quest to invent the light bulb. After many failures, he said *"I have only discovered ways in which it may not be done!"* The more failures he made, the closer he thought he approached the solution. What an attitude!

It is your responsibility to remove all the clutter from your mind so you can see clearly your dream. You have to see it within in order to see it without.

Every one of us has a distraction specifically designed to keep us from achieving our potential. It could be a habit, a weakness, fear of the future, disappointment with our past, or our 'busyness' in our daily schedules. Everything clouding your vision within has to be done away with. The achievement of your dream is dependent on your ability to first see clearly your vision within, and then to hold it firmly in your spirit until it materialises. Your dream must become the blueprint within so you can see it manifest on the outside. You also need to be at peace within yourself so you can have the concentration to pursue your dream. If you feel cluttered within, begin to put things in order in your life and there's no end to the potential benefits.

It would amaze you to know the number of people you are better off than. Be thankful, for many would give an arm to have what you have.

Maintaining an attitude of gratitude and being thankful for what you have is the easiest way to eliminate worry from your life. Ingratitude paves the way to a complaining attitude; and a complaining attitude will destroy your potential. You don't have to look far to see how blessed you are. You most probably have clean water to drink, and are spoilt for choice with what to eat. Many people are dying daily for need of some of the basic things we take for granted; and in many more places than one, you would be classified a millionaire! Eric Hoffer said of gratitude, *"The hardest arithmetic to master is that which enables us to count our blessings!"* Get into the habit of counting your blessings and it really would surprise you to know how well-off you are.

Learn to see everyone's uniqueness through the eyes of God's immense ability. Everyone is a blueprint of success and is inimitable in their personality.

Learning to be tolerant of everyone is essential. In our pursuits, we come across many people with different personalities which we may shun because they are not like us. But personality is the sum total of a person's mental, spiritual and physical traits and habits that distinguish him from *ALL OTHERS!* So it is not very prudent to ask why the other person is not just like you. If they were, there would not be the need for you anyway, because someone just like you would have come and accomplished your purpose long ago. Our uniqueness colours the spectrum of life and makes it more interesting. So instead of being critical of other people's inability to 'be like you', choose rather, to see them through their uniqueness.

Life is like chess. It takes long moments of strategising, planning and action to conquer.

Winning in life takes something more than just 'going with the flow.' It is said that 'if we fail to plan, we plan to fail.' Do not underestimate the importance of planning. When you engage in systematic, purposeful action, using goals and making wise choices, stretching your abilities to the maximum, you cannot help but feel positive and confident about yourself. Napoleon Hill once said, *"Every well built house started in the form of a definite purpose plus a definite plan in the nature of a set of blueprints."*

You can achieve success if only you are prepared to do what it takes to achieve it! It does not come through wishing, but through careful planning and action.

Purpose in your mind to stop *'going with the flow'* and start planning to live your life!

Look within not without.

One of the greatest weights you can shed off your back is depending on others. When you get used to depending on others, you inhibit your creativity and stifle your growth process. Certain things in life come our way to cause growth in us but we lose this potential benefit when all we do is run to others for help. Yes, no man is an island and we need each other; but personal growth is dependent on your ability to face life squarely. No one in life has the ability to lift you to the place you belong except the person you see in the mirror every morning. Meet your greatest helper and miracle worker, next to God; You!

Luck is spelt W-O-R-K.

Luck is one word not found in the dictionary of a proactive person, driven to the achievement of his vision. They never believe in luck and circumstances but rather in cause and effect. They understand that if their desires are going to materialise, they are going to have to engage in purposeful action. People who believe in luck and hope in 'lady luck', live by default and not by design, waiting for someone or something good to come their way. Samuel Goldwyn, founder of MGM said *"The harder I work, the luckier I get."* He could not have been more precise.

Life is a hyphen locked between two dates. It is the gap between two confirmed appointments – birth and death. A successful life is one that overshadows the enormity of these two certain events.

I recently attended the funeral of a prominent man I knew. On his tombstone was written the birth and death dates, with a tiny dash locked between them. What the little dash represents is what the ink of our lives so indelibly writes in the pages of our history, daily. We sometimes need to ask ourselves some tough questions like, "what will I be remembered for when my time comes? What will that little dash represent? Will my life be celebrated, my deeds missed, and my loss mourned?" Today, you can begin to re-write your history. It's never too late.

Man is a unique being capable of achieving anything within the limits of his imagination. The broader your imagination, the more your ideas and the greater things you can achieve. For all earned wealth have their source in an idea.

Have you ever sat down to figure out why man was endowed with an imagination? I believe the imagination is the gateway to the realm of possibilities. It is said that *whatever the mind of man can conceive and believe, it can achieve.* Yet, the imagination is one of the most under-utilised abilities of man. The achievement of any dream is never possible until it is first conceived and then believed. When you conceive a dream within, it embeds itself in your subconscious mind, making incredible resources available to you. Build the habit of taking time off to dream.

Most of us do not place demands on the incredible sources of greatness within us, waiting to be unearthed. Our efforts are sometimes so weak that they make no impression on our creative energies.

Jack Schwartz, American expert in human potential said, *"We are hoarding potentials so great that they are just about unimaginable."* We are like deep wells full of water, with the ability to supply endless amounts of water. Also, Jean Houston said, *"We all have the extraordinary coded within us…waiting to be released."* We are all 'Greatness embodied', waiting to metamorphose into reality. The issue confronting us now is how to tap into our incredible resources in order to elevate our lives by conscious endeavour. All the great men we have known, who grazed the 'corridors of prominence' with their lives, first had a dream. Then they believed that the only person capable of getting them there was themselves. Place a demand on yourself to discover the real you, and you will be amazed the incredible wealth at your disposal.

Begin with the end in mind; plan how to get there and then take action. This is the three step formula to achieving anything in life.

This three step formula is essential to the achievement of anything in life. Many times we set goals and resolutions very excitedly but never devise an adequate plan to keep the goal alive. What you achieve by planning is that you bring the future into the present so that you can so something about it now. But even then, we have to take action by living the plan, before we can achieve the goal. It is said that *"planning without action is futile; action without planning is fatal!"* Today, revisit your goals and resolutions and see if this formula is yielding the results you desire.

Much activity does not imply resourcefulness or results. Ensure that your activities are in line with your goals.

We live in the days of the 'mad rush'. Everyone seems to be running and dashing after something, without stopping to catch a breath. Some believe that the more things they can get their teeth into, the more effective they will be. But it is easy to be busy and yet not be effective. If you are perpetually busy, you are not more effective than an idle man. Henry David Thoreau once said, *"It is not enough to be busy; so are the ants. The question is: What are we busy about?"* If you feel caught in the trap of 'busyness', it's time to take a step back to assess your much activity against your vision and goals.

No amount of external influence has enough power to assassinate the vision of a focused man for he holds the dream within. But if he opens the gates to his soul by reacting negatively to the external pressures, then he loses focus.

The doors to change and the doors to our vision can only be opened from within. It is true that there are many things in life that seek to distract our attention from our focus. But none of those things possess any power in themselves to achieve their purpose unless we grant them access by our reaction. How we choose to react to any situation determines its effect over us and that is why it is absolutely important that we consciously and consistently protect our vision from every influence by choosing to react in a way that will not destroy our focus.

Scars may be ugly but they provide a source of energy and determination to the bearer that drives him to more than make up for the wrong decisions that led to his mistakes.

Failure and disappointing experiences tend to leave scars on us emotionally. Their effect on our emotions is however, dependent upon us. They can either be a catalyst for progress or a hammock we rest our future in. I have realised that people with a great capacity for living and a determination to achieve purpose are not stopped by their mistakes. They keep pressing on even though many may see them through the scars of their past. If you find yourself in a position today where your drive for the future has been arrested by your past, let go of it and run. Use your scars as a springboard into your future. You can do it, if you really want to.

The best guide you could have in your communication with others is to keep in mind that we all perceive things differently. That is what makes us unique. Do not be peeved when others do not see things the way you see them.

One thing that colours the spectrum of life is the uniqueness of our being. No two people that exist or have ever existed on this earth are the same. Our individual uniqueness is what led to the need for the concept of agreement. If we were all the same, there would not have been the need to agree. Further to this, even twins, raised under the same environment turn out different. I have often wondered why people complain that others are not like them, or why they do not see things the way they see them. We are all different, and one mark of maturity is learning to adapt to our differences. When you have this understanding, you learn to appreciate others for who they are. This is the key to harmony in our relationships.

The biggest plus about mistakes and failures is that they show you how NOT to do things.

Failure is a temporary setback that should cause you to rethink your position, focus and strategy. It is nothing to be afraid of. Yes, I do agree that it is uncomfortable to fail in an attempt. But when failure does come your way, it is important to perceive it rightly so you can gain from it, the wisdom and knowledge to launch out again rightly. It is also important to realise that you are not the same as your failure. It is only an event. Perhaps, you find yourself in a place where your wrong perspective of failure is keeping you from becoming the best you were created to be. You are greater than your failures.

The man who fails in a venture and does not re-evaluate nor take account of the steps that led to failure in his last try, is surely bound to make the same mistake again. For if you do things the way you've always done them, you're bound to achieve the same results.

One of the greatest benefits of failure is that it presents us with an opportunity to start again with the experiences and wisdom learned from our previously failed attempt. But if you refuse to evaluate your mistakes before launching out again, you will miss out on the opportunity for the growth embedded within the experience. It's all about your attitude to life. You must be determined not to repeat the mistakes, and to maximise the seeds of the equivalent benefits from what is learned in the process. You cannot go on applying the same process that led you to your mistakes and expect to get a different result. That just doesn't work. If you want to see a different result than what you got, then you must be willing to do something different from what you've always done!

Enthusiasm is the energy that keeps you pushing towards your goal. Have loads of it, for sometimes the journey is uphill.

If there is any quality truly necessary for the achievement of one's purpose, it is enthusiasm. Enthusiasm is the passion or burning desire within one about a particular endeavour or pursuit. The word enthusiasm comes from the Greek word, *entheos* which means *'God within'*. I like to describe an enthusiastic man as one who knows that he knows that his God lives within him, to enable him do the impossible. So he runs with excitement that never grows cold. It is the source of that boundless energy that keeps you running when everything seems to be against you. Above all, what enthusiasm does is, it releases within you, the drive to carry you over obstacles and adds significance to all you do. Charles M Schwab said, *"A man can succeed at almost anything for which he has unlimited enthusiasm."* There is no better time than now to regain the fire and passion for our dreams. Get excited about your life!

The strength of your character is what will determine the security of your reputation. You can spend a lifetime building a reputation but without a foundation of good character, be certain of this one thing – it shall not remain for long.

We have been conditioned to pursue success and good reputation without giving heed to the important foundation of character. For example, some would go to great lengths to achieve a particular aim without a thought of who could get hurt, cheated, or destroyed. Integrity is not a popular word these days. *"You have to be fast...."* is what we're advised. A man's character is the reality of himself while his reputation is how people see him. And because of this, reputation can be shattered after one careless moment. Your reputation will change based on how people see you because your reputation is held in the hands of others. Character on the other hand, is the true substance of 'who you are', which is not affected by anything external. When built on, it reveals true substance in everything you do. Are you pursuing success based on true character?

There is a healthy fear called apprehension which goes hand in hand with exploring new territory. Don't allow the anticipation of apprehension to prevent you from achieving your dream or taking on new challenges.

Daring to step out of your comfort zone into unchartered territory takes courage and some guts. I personally do not believe people who claim they felt no fear when they dared to step out. Know this one thing that courage is not the absence of fear but the ability to act regardless of the fear. It is not denying the fearful obstacles staring at you but daring to believe that something on the inside of you is superior to circumstance. *Sir Edmund Hillary* made several attempts to scale Mount Everest before succeeding. After one such attempt he stood at the base of the mountain, shook his fist in defiance and shouted, *'I'll defeat you yet; you're as big as you're going to get, but I'm still growing!'* He went on to succeed in climbing the mountain. Greatness comes at a high price and not by some stroke of luck. Don't be a *'play-it-safer'* because of fear or you will never know how great and influential you could have been

There is always a way to get your lifestyle to fit your means and still have some excess. It is a skill many have not mastered yet. It is called moderation.

Living in moderation is probably one of the most disciplined things to do. Moderation in itself denotes living with restraint and self-control, and by being able to deny yourself some pleasures now which would become affordable later. Many of us have found ourselves in debt because we have not known how to 'live on a little', and have become slaves to debtors. I am not suggesting to you not to desire a better life but to ensure that every inch along the way to our wealthy place, we keep our passions which crave for instant gratification under control. Before you decide to acquire anything, you MUST first of all ask yourself the following:

- Do I really need it?
- What would happen if I did not get this?
- Are there any alternatives to this?
- Could I invest the money somewhere more profitable for my tomorrow?

And above all this, develop a budget and do whatever it takes to keep your outgoings within its constraints.

To fulfil your potential, you must be committed to growth; and growth is not always comfortable.

The process of discovering one's potential involves a great deal of learning and courage to step into the unknown; and wherever there is learning, there is growth. By default, we all grow older with time but we must endeavour to channel our growth into maximising our potential. This is the kind of growth that comes by choice and is challenging to do. In five years, we shall be five years older but some of us will have something more than a +5 to our age. We would have put ourselves through some rigorous learning processes that induced growth in line with our potential. That is what true growth is about – maximising time to be the best that one was created to be. Former American President Calvin Coolidge said, *"All growth depends on activity. There is no development physically or intellectually without effort, and effort means WORK!"* If we do purposeful work, we shall achieve our potential, and live a full life.

We all have an inherent need to be appreciated by others. But when we allow this need to become dominant in our character and relationships, we lose our joy.

Everyone has a part of them that desires to be appreciated by others, either for something done, or to simply feel valued. This inherent part of us becomes an issue when it becomes our motivation for action. I have seen people's emotions become so dependent on receiving praise and acceptance from others that they lost their own sense of worth. I have seen other people who stopped giving service in Church because the Pastor or someone did not appreciate them for what they do. It always leads to bitterness and hurt because what effectively happens is that you place your joy and sense of worth in other people's hands. In life, the greatest value anyone can place on you should never come close in magnitude to the value you place on yourself. Don't let your joy rest in the hands of others. Begin to value yourself.

You may not have been responsible for the things that happened to you in your childhood, but your future is in your hands.

There are essentially two stages in our lives: childhood and adulthood. These stages are not distinguished by age alone, but by something more important – Choice. As children, we are usually products of our environment as we cannot choose where to live or what to do. Everything is more or less decided for us. On the other hand, adults are people who realise that their lives are products of choice and that what they do today will ultimately determine what comes their way tomorrow. The transition from childhood to adulthood truly happens in one's life when they consciously make the decision to live by choice, irrespective of what the past presented to them when they were products of their environment. Listen, your future has nothing to do with your past, absolutely nothing. Rather, it has everything to do with today and what you choose to do with it. Take responsibility now and do something positive with your life!

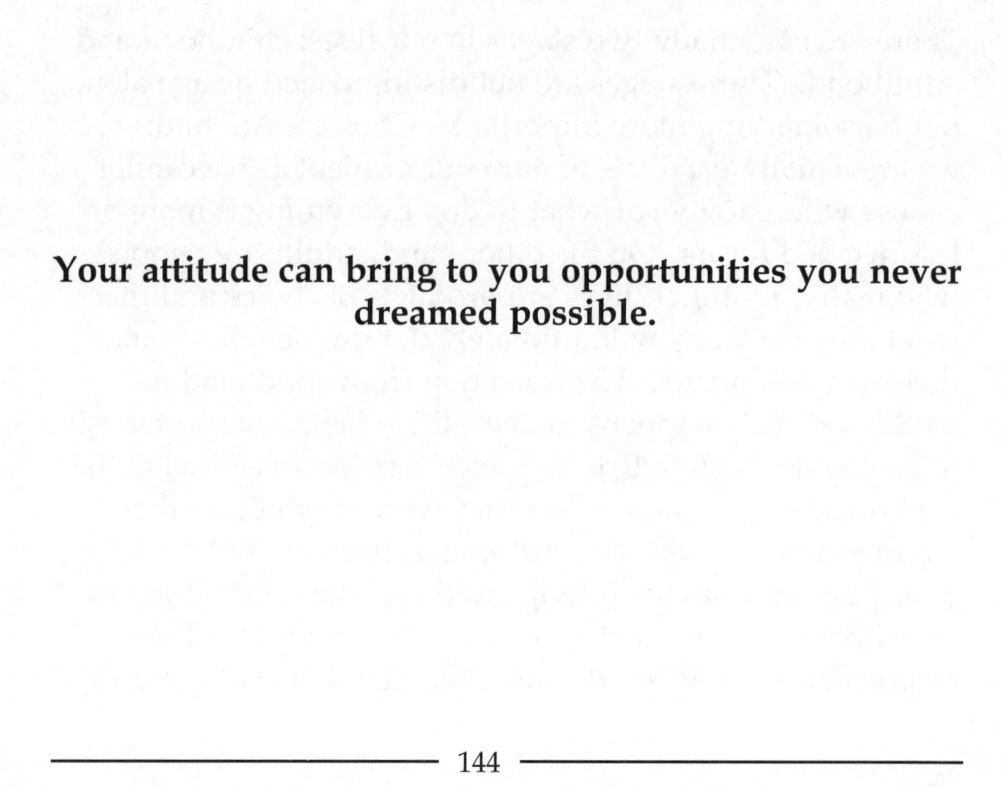

Your attitude can bring to you opportunities you never dreamed possible.

Every sailor will agree that, irrespective of the gales that blow at sea, it is not the gales that determine the direction they go but the set of sails mounted. The same can be said of life and that is, it is not the pressures of life that should determine our progress but our attitude and effort. Though opportunities come to us all, those with a positive outlook on life tend to have more opportunities in life. Why? Because as H. Jackson Brown Jr. puts it in his 'Life's Little Instruction Book', *"opportunity dances with those who are ready on the dance floor!"* And this, my friends, is the attitude to adopt. Attitude, as is said, is a little thing that makes a big difference.

Your thoughts and imagination have the ability to keep you captive. But even more do they have the ability to give you the freedom to be who you were created to be.

Because of the profound effect of your thoughts on your behaviour and outlook on life, you need to cultivate a healthy thought pattern. If all that your thoughts dwell on are the difficulties in life and the disappointment of your failed attempts, then the fruit of those seeds is what you are going to get from life. But if you choose to believe that you can do it; that life can and will get better some day, even though your today has no bearing with that thought, life will change. Opportunities will come your way and you will begin to cultivate ideas you never thought about. The first century Roman Emperor, Marcus Aurelius said, *"Very little is needed to make a happy life; it is all within yourself, in the way of thinking."* Thoughts, are powerful. Use them wisely. Think 'can-can!'

Your perception in every situation is absolutely essential. Your perception is derived from who your experiences in life have made you; for your experiences in life create the lenses through which you see and define everything. This implies that the way you see a thing or define a situation may be true to you but not necessarily the truth.

How you see a thing is vital to your interpretation of it. Your perception is that mechanism by which you interpret information received through your senses. It is formed through your experiences and works like a mirror that reflects your state of mind outward. Therefore, you see things as you are and not necessarily as they are. Former British author, Penelope Fitzgerald said, *"No two people see the external world in exactly the same way. To every separate person, a thing is what he thinks it is; in other words, not a thing but a think."* When you understand this fact, you will learn to be more tolerant of the views of others. But more importantly, analyse your perceptions and get a better perspective of them. It will go a long way to help you judge situations rightly.

Today well lived and spent profitably in pursuit of your dream will make you look on your yesterdays with joy and to your tomorrows with hope.

Have you experienced the elation that goes with accomplishing everything you set out to do on a particular day? There is a certain feel-good factor that comes when you spend a day profitably and achieve everything you planned to. This feel-good factor has an enormous effect on your personal motivation. It increases your motivation and makes you confident. Most importantly, it makes you feel in control of your destiny because you understand that what you do today culminates in the happenings of tomorrow. You are responsible for what you are; and today, you have the power to make yourself whatever you desire to be. So what really matters is today and how you decide to live it. For however you decide to live it will result in either getting you closer or further from the realisation of your dream.

Your thoughts have a special mechanism wherewith they attract situations congruent with your thought pattern.

James Allen made a stunning statement when he enlightened us that our lives are what our thoughts make them; and that a man will find that as he alters his thoughts towards things and other people, things and other people will alter towards him. Have you ever been in the situation where you started thinking good thoughts about someone you disliked, and soon saw a change in the attitude of the person? Or have you thought and desired a thing so badly that opportunities showed up? Good and bad alike? Our thoughts are like seeds. When we sow them, they germinate and bear fruit. Begin to think good thoughts and you will be amazed at the sudden change that will spring in your life.

Hope is the lifeline that keeps us from being swept away in life's storms.

Orison Swett Marden said of hope that *"There is no medicine like hope, no incentive so great, and no tonic so powerful as expectation of something tomorrow."* There are some pretty tough times life brings our way at some point in our lives, and in such times, you are going to need something that makes you see beyond the situation. You see, hope will give you strength to endure today with the promise of a better tomorrow. Hope will anchor your soul to the belief that what you expect will come when this storm passes. Do not let your hopes die because of the delayed manifestation of what you hope for. It may wane but keep it alive, and it will never fail you.

We are this minute a decision away from starting to realise who we really are, and what we are capable of.

When I was a child, I used to depend on the impetus of New Year's Eve to give me the much needed drive to embark on changing certain things in my life. I would pledge to myself many things I would accomplish the following year but would however find myself shipwrecked after a couple of months. And when this happened, I would console myself and wait for the next New Year's Eve to begin again! I did not know that at any point in time, I could begin again. One of the greatest truths about life is that any moment can be a starting point, irrespective of how many times you have tried and failed. The journey to discover yourself, which is your first calling to help you fulfil your unique purpose, can start this very moment if you will only decide to. Make a firm decision right now to maximise your life!